THE SMART MOMS GUIDE TO SOFTWARE TESTING

You can work in Tech (Yes, You)

No Coding. No going back to School. How Moms Can Build a Flexible, Remote Career in Software Testing

Jennifer Barbour

2/6/2026

Dedication

This book is dedicated to my 4 reasons for living: My husband Justin and my 3 children I love to infinity and beyond.

Disclaimer

This book was written by me, not AI. I love tech but I won't let AI replace my words.

Table of Contents

PROLOGUE

A Letter to Working Mothers

Dear fellow mommas,

As I sit here writing this book, I am filled with nervousness as well as excitement. I am a mother of 3, and just like you, juggling the demands of my family, my career and a house that never seems to stay clean. It's a journey that can sometimes feel overwhelming, but having to choose between sacrificing your professional aspirations or spending time with your family should not be an option.

Through my own experience I have discovered a career path that not only provides professional fulfillment, but also offers the flexibility and work-life balance that as mothers we yearn for. That gem is <u>Software Testing</u>, also known as Software QA (Quality Assurance) and it has opened doors of opportunity and growth in my life that I hope may do the same for you, and just FYI I don't code, I love tech but not programming haha.

I remembered my daughter asking me the other day, "Did you know what you wanted to be when you were my age?" and I replied "Yes I did" because in my mind I remembered always liking gadgets, buttons, screens or any type of computer and also always noticing "defects" in movies, I had a detective eye, but her next line made me laugh, she said "Really? So when you were 6 you were like 'I can't wait to be in meetings all day?'" I couldn't stop laughing at her response because it made me realize my kids have no idea what I do for a living, they just know it involves computers and meetings.

It really made me think about why it is that I love my career field, it seems so boring from the eyes of a child and I sure as hell did not wish to be in meetings all day, but the answer was clear,

Software Testing was my childhood dream, it involved computers like I've always liked, gadgets (whatever device you need to test will be sent by the company, ex: tablets, phones, laptops, TV's, game consoles, smart glasses, etc.), It involves using your detective skills on a daily basis, it beat the long commute to the office, the pay was great, and I got to watch my kids grow, especially my baby that I was still breastfeeding during those meetings. If I had to work on-site I would've had to pump every 2 hours and as most working mamas know, it's not a very comfortable situation (I worked on site with my first 2 kids), in fact some companies don't even offer "maternity rooms" at an acceptable standard (Yes I've had to pump in bathrooms before), and thanks to my daughter's "observation" I switched to a new job that has almost no meetings.

That's one of the many beauties about Software Testing, you are never stuck at any job if you don't want to be and you can test for entirely different industries (Gaming, Healthcare, Banking, E-commerce?) whatever you find more interesting. In these pages, I want to share with you the reasons why software testing is an ideal career choice for working moms. I want to break the stereotypes, debunk the myths, and show you how this field just might be what you were looking for to find that perfect balance.

We will delve into the world of software testing and discover the flexible work arrangements, the intellectual challenges, and the opportunities for growth that await us. We will uncover the transferable skills gained through motherhood that make us particularly qualified to succeed in this industry. So, dear mommas, let's embark on this journey together.

With love,

Jennifer

INTRODUCTION

About the Author

Who am I? I'm a 20+ year tester and counting. No, I am not 20 years old (maybe in mind, haha), but I have over 20 years of experience in this career field.

I have worked in 3 states, in almost every industry you can imagine, testing everything from games, websites, and software apps, to government classified information, you name it! I've worked for small start-ups and Fortune 500 companies, some of which include Mattel, DirecTV, Chevron, PlutoTV, among others.

I have learned a lot over the past decades I could have never learned in school, things I wish I knew when I was younger, things only experience can teach, and things that scared me to death and later figured out I was overwhelmed and intimidated for no good reason.

My name is Jennifer Barbour, I'm married and a mother of a boy and 2 girls, a dog and a cat, living my dream life in Houston, Texas, writing this in my pajamas. It wasn't always this comfortable. I grew up in South America in a little country called Ecuador (you know, the middle of the world). I came to the US at 17, and had to learn English fast before graduation to make it into college. Once I enrolled, I had to figure out how to pay for it (I hate debt, so I never accepted loans) and learn to survive as an adult. I won't go into a full biography (maybe that's a topic for another book called "the struggle is real" haha), but let's just say if I made it and have a successful tech career, as a woman, as a minority and with English as my second language then so can you!

I hope my journey will help answer some of the most common questions about Software Testing. There is nothing more frustrating than not knowing what to learn next, or even worse, having a long list of things to learn only to discover later that you didn't really need to know all that stuff.

This book will help you make your personal "to learn" list as accurate as possible. Once you know your end goal and which path to follow, your dream becomes a realistic objective, and there's nothing more exciting than knowing how to get there.

I want to remove all the fluff and help you learn just what you need about the type of testing you want to do. I am by no means a 'know it all' and will try and write this book mostly with my own words, not with definitions from Wikipedia or AI, so it's easier to understand.

I want this book to feel like I'm conversing with a friend about my job experience and giving as much advice as possible. I don't want it to be another computer textbook you picked out at the library that leaves you with more questions than answers and assumes you already know everything.

I hope this book will be everything I wished I had when I was just starting in this career field and can positively affect and change the lives of other aspiring Testers. Software Testing is an exciting career field with many opportunities and freedoms, I can't wait to show you!

What You Will Learn

Mainly, this book helps you choose your path. The computer industry has many branches and career fields (Developers, Engineers, Architects, Testers.) there are so many options it's hard to know which one to follow if you simply love computers.

Each one of those computer fields has its specialties and branches. This book will concentrate on the many paths related to Software Testing. In this field alone, we have different specialties, and it can get overwhelming if you don't know which one to focus on, especially if you believe Software Testing is just one broad field covering everything QA (Quality Assurance) related.

That's what I used to think, and I'd overwork myself trying to learn different apps, software and acronyms, all just to read a job description that named a new list of words I've never heard before. Made me realize I never meet half the requirements listed. I thought, "OMG, I will never find a job in this field because it's always changing!"

I'd read job postings where the title would be "Software Test Engineer," and the description would say "Do performance testing," and I would feel lost and think, "What is that? I do manual testing. Is performance testing a different thing?" And then read the requirements, which listed software I've never used before. It made me think, "After so many years in testing, I'm still missing requirements?"

So I'd write down the requirements and then learn them one at a time. Then, after I felt confident, I'd add it all to my resume and then search for a job again, only to find the same title but a different job description and a new list of requirements I wasn't familiar with again, bringing me back to step 1, repeatedly.

The more I learned about something, the more I got myself into a rabbit hole and followed a different path than I was originally trying to reach. The job descriptions weren't changing; I was just not looking at the right job for me.

I finally learned the hard way there are many different testers, and that most recruiters and companies that write the job descriptions don't know that, so they title the ad "Searching for a Software Tester," but rarely do they list the specialty. For example, "Searching for a Performance Tester" is how it should be. I finally learned that I just needed to concentrate on the jobs that needed the testing I did, which at the time was mostly Frontend Manual Testing.

There are different career paths INSIDE this field, and it's very easy to steer from the end goal by getting confused (almost tricked) into learning unnecessary things. Things that later, you find out are just used in one type of testing that you're not even interested in doing.

This book will teach you what you need to learn. I won't teach you how to program in JAVA, use Selenium or Jira or Bugzilla. I will teach you whether or not you NEED to learn those things based on the testing career you choose.

Think of this book as a big cheat sheet, as if someone in college told you exactly what the teacher will ask about in the exam, it's up to you to do the research and study the answers.

The hardest part was always figuring out the WHAT, not the HOW.

Once you know WHAT you need to learn, the HOW will come easy as it's just a Google away.

I will teach you that if you see a job description that says you need to know automation and then lists "Selenium, Cucumber,

QC ALM" in the requirements, it doesn't mean you need to know all those applications. They pretty much do the same thing; it means you need to know ONE.

Testing jobs love to list all synonyms in the requirements, much like keywords, just so their ad appears in your search or so it's easier for them to find a candidate.

For example, if you know how to use Jira to write defects and the job requires you to know Spira, guess what, you can tell them on the cover letter, "well I don't know Spira, but I've used Jira (or any of the many other defect logging apps available)," and you will probably get at least an interview because all those apps are used similarly. Once you know one, it's easy to learn another one. Then, you can be trained on the job on the specifics of the software they use.

Remember, companies don't hire just based on what you know. They hire based on "Potential," whether you will be easy to train and adjust. So the more you already know, the easier your learning curve will be.

The best way to start is with a magic word I like to call FOCUS, choose one path and learn everything about that specialty. Remember, light spread through a magnifying glass from far away doesn't do much but, focused on the right distance, turns into a laser light that can start a fire. Even water can cut metal when its force is pressurized through a tiny hole.

Focusing on one path is the way to become an expert. Now, if you choose to specialize in more than one type of testing later, even better. You'll have a lot more opportunities open up, remember to focus on one goal at a time.

PART I

What is Software Testing?

Software Testing is a phase in the SDLC (Software Development Life Cycle) where Testers have to find defects, irregularities, and anything that doesn't meet requirements. We go by many names: Software Testers, Quality Assurance Testers, Software Test Engineers, Software Analysts, QA Analysts, Quality Control Analysts, and a mix and match of all of the above, which makes it hard to look for work sometimes.

Sounds like a simple enough job doesn't it? Someone else makes the software while we just break it. Well, in order to break it you need to use some special tools and different kinds of software. Unfortunately for us, seems every company out there uses different applications, which is why I had to write my other book "Choosing the right Software Testing Career" where I specifically go over the different types of testing and what software you need to learn to do each. That way you don't learn something you don't need to and waste time. (By the way I'm copying and pasting everything from my first book here so you don't have to buy that one too)

Basically Software Testing is the final step before a product goes live, and you give it that final seal of approval. Recently I've seen more specified titles in job listings, which is good. Once you know the tester you want to be, you can just search for that specialty. For example, "Accessibility Tester" or "Automation Tester," or "Performance" or "Security" tester, and although the results will be far less than when doing a general "Software Tester" search, you will be more likely to meet most requirements and land an interview.

Why Software Testing is an Ideal Career Choice for Mothers

I know how Tech jobs sound intimidating, some people think they are not good with "computers" and can't fathom the idea of working in Software, but let me tell you something, if you are a mother, then you have super powers and you are more than qualified for this position, the best part? You don't even need to learn how to code.

Now yes there are types of testing that require programming skills, something you can learn in 6 months if you have the time to immerse yourself in YouTube or an online course, BUT if you barely have time to eat or sleep like I do, then programming isn't an option and you are better off doing the types of testing that don't require it.

With that said, why do I think this is THE job for moms? Because of the freedom it gives you. No one needs to be able to walk away from a computer 100 times a day like moms do, no one loses focus every 5 minutes due to a random interruption by a little creature like moms do, no one has to worry about laundry, dinner, dishes and pet feeding like moms do, and on top of all the household work, who can afford to live on one income nowadays?

Software Testing is the answer, because you can do it remotely, you can do it on your own time, you can be interrupted constantly and continue where you left at any moment, the pay is great, and there's not a ton of competition, I mean, how many Software Testers have you met in your lifetime?.

Now when it comes to job security, it's not THAT secure, meaning companies will let you go the minute they think their site is bug-free, which is also why a lot of testing jobs are short contracts (As I'm writing this book, I'm on my 13th job) no job is forever, layoffs will become your best friend and you'll see them for what they are, an opportunity to grow, an opportunity to learn a new type of software, and an opportunity for a raise.

The type of job security that I'm talking about means you will always be on high demand, even in the age of AI, manual testers are still needed. All companies need testers, all industries need testers. Where there is software, there is a need for someone to test it. There are more jobs out there than there are testers, which Is why I'm writing this book, I can't do it all alone hahaha.

Common Misconceptions about Software Testing

Myth #1 Software Jobs are mostly for men and computer geniuses

What's the first thing that comes to mind when you hear Software Testing? you automatically think "Computer nerd" or "Tech savvy" either one sounds a bit difficult to achieve. Well, it's neither.

I know the word Software is intimidating, especially for women. People think software jobs are hard and they are mostly for men, which is not true, now yes there are mostly men working in I.T related fields but over my 20 year career in this field, I can tell you those demographics are changing quickly.

Back in the day (2000 - 2005 with breaks in between) when I worked at Mattel we were 72 testers, guess how many of us were girls?

THREE! that's right... out of 72 game testers, only 3 of us were female. Now fast forward to 2023, my current job is testing corporate websites, I am one of 10 or so testers and I'll say its about 50/50 male and female. I have certainly met more female testers in the last decade than ever before and I love it! I love having more female co-workers that can relate, especially moms. So don't be scared, if I can do it, you can do it, I am by no means a computer genius.

Myth #2 I need to know how to code

This for me is one of the best myths to debunk. Programming skills have never been my forte. I have tried JAVA, Python, C# and I hated them all the same. I thought I would be out of a job as I kept seeing more and more "Automation tester" jobs out there, which yes those positions are quickly becoming the majority, but when I took a hard look at all the types of testing there is, I simply decided not to go for Automation.

You can literally type "manual tester" or "Manual QA" on LinkedIn and see tons of job postings. Don't get me wrong if you learn how to code you can make some big bucks, automation testers can earn anywhere from $60 to $100 per hour but for me the stress that it required, the amount of focus to write scripts, and attention to detail you have to put into the code, just wasn't worth the extra cash.

I always chased the money but the more I wanted, the less freedom I actually had. I remember trying to write code in JAVA and every time I ran the script I kept getting errors. I missed a dot somewhere, I forgot to add a space between that random character and that other one that for me make no sense, I missed a colon or quote mark somewhere and it ruined the whole thing, I just hated writing in code, I preferred plain English.

I Actually did some automation testing for one of my jobs but I did not enjoy it. There were delays in testing because the code wasn't ready, it had nothing to do with the software being bad, most of the errors found were "code" related. I didn't have time to find actual defects because I was wasting time getting the scripts right, I found it to be stressful and just not practical.

I thought: isn't this what developers are for? They code, I never wanted to be a developer and it felt like I was quickly turning into one. So I decided that whenever I'd look for a job I would specify the type of testing I'm more comfortable with. I took a course on Automation testing, I passed, I could do it if I reeaaaally wanted to, but the amount of stress it gave me just made me want to go back to manual.

Myth #3 Manual testers are disappearing

Simply not true. You don't "NEED" to learn how to code if you don't want to. Again, if you do, great! It is never a bad thing to know more or learn extra skills, but do it as long as you enjoy it. Remember if you hate the course you're taking, how are you going to like working on it full time? If you enjoy the course, you'll enjoy the job.

One thing that's for sure is you have to keep up with technology though. Just because you don't like to code doesn't mean companies aren't going for automation, they will hire an automation tester as well as a manual one to work side by side.

There are tools that you can use that don't use code and now with the help of AI we can automate a lot of our work flow.

Also there are specific jobs for people that code, like SDET's (Software Development Engineer in Test), which is basically a tester that turned into a developer or a developer that turned tester. There's Automation Engineers which are testers that code or Software Engineers that test but basically they write automated scripts which complement Manual testing.

Let me give you some basic reasons why Manual testing isn't going away:

Human Judgment and Exploratory Testing: When checking software, manual testers use their judgment, intuition, and creativity, which is helpful for spotting complicated and unexpected problems that automated tests could overlook. We call this Exploratory Testing.

User Experience: Manual testers can evaluate software from a user's point of view by examining things like usability, accessibility and user-friendliness. Delivering a positive user experience depends on having a thorough understanding of how users interact with software. We need to make mistakes, we need to test like a user that does NOT know how to use the software, we need to be random. Only humans can make human mistakes, this is part of Usability Testing.

New and Evolving Software: Agile development involves frequent software modifications. Because manual testing is flexible and responsive to changes, it's more appropriate for projects with constant updates and requirement changes (which believe me, happen more often than not)

Complex animations, interactive elements: Many websites nowadays have interactive elements, things that appear on click like pop ups, modals, links that open new tabs, tables, sorting and filtering, dropdown menus with selectable items like checkboxes or bullets. A lot of tests that involve complex functionality are usually missed or failed by Automated tests. Sometimes even a slow response (ex: suggested results when you do a search) can take forever to appear and that would cause an automated test to fail, when in reality it's just a slow server and you have to keep adjusting the timing on the scripts until it gets it right.

For example I'm currently working as an Accessibility Tester and the developers run all these automated tests before the page even gets to me, then I find twice the amount of defects the automated tests found, why? Because some things appear with specific interactions, like for example the automated scan missed an X or "close" button that only appeared after a user enters info on a form, this button was read by the screen reader as "Zero". By the way if you don't know what Accessibility testing or screen readers are no worries, I'm not giving a class on Software Testing right now, I'm just using examples letting you know that manual testing is crucial for any type of Software Development.

Myth #4 Manual testers will never earn a 6 figure salary.

Nothing is further from the truth. It all depends on experience and the type of testing you want to do, for example a game tester that mostly just checks functionality will usually earn less than an Accessibility Tester or Performance Tester (neither requires coding, it helps but it's not mandatory). Different industries pay differently, I know I was making more as a manual tester for 3 different jobs (testing for a streaming app, testing a corporate website, and testing for healthcare) All 3 paid a 6 figure salary, which was more than my friends doing Automated Testing working for the Government. (Government jobs will always pay lower in my experience).

Now a Manual QA can reach (keep in mind.. I'm saying 'reach' not 'start') a 6 figure salary easily and quickly, Starting at entry level with zero experience, if you have a college degree especially in a computer or engineering field, you can start with $25 to $35 per hour.

With no degree but some experience (at least 2 years) you're in the higher $30's, and once you add at least 5 years experience and a couple of certifications, you can start at $50 per hour and voila! 6 figure salary.

Myth #5 You need a Computer Science degree

How do you get your foot in the door if you have no degree and no experience? You can take online computer courses on a specific type of testing and get certified. There are Accessibility Testing courses (and certifications), there's Automated Testing courses (and different certifications), I for example learned Performance testing in 2 months and got a certification, I didn't like it so I never tried getting a job in it but I could have. Companies want you to know how to use the software (tools) used to run whatever type of testing they require. You have to learn how to use the tools.

What if you want to work as a tester before you get a certification? I will teach you the basics of testing so you can at least have a decent conversation with a recruiter and be familiar with the terms.

I started working as a video game tester while I was going to college, so I didn't have a degree nor any certifications at the time, all they required was a High School diploma.

Once my foot was in the door, it was easy to get my next job, I switched from gaming to e-commerce and then websites, software applications, and even streaming apps. It's not hard to switch, companies don't want previous experience with their industry or their field, they want previous experience with testing, they don't care what it is you tested. With 5+ yrs of experience you can earn $35 to $65 per hour as a manual tester and the best part, you can do it all from the comfort of your home once you have that experience under your belt.

Who is this Career For?

When you were a child, did you ever think, "I can't wait to grow up and be a Software Tester?" Probably not, but we didn't know what we would be called. I always knew I'd work with computers. I just didn't know what exactly I'd be doing.

This career is perfect for people with a passion for gadgets, technology, and the latest inventions. For people that notice defects in everything (from household products to TV shows and movies) and are not afraid to bring them up, and people that like to "test" different things out, like you use a different type of deodorant or shampoo every time one finishes, until you find one you love.

If you have a good eye for spotting mistakes, if you were a kid that loved those handheld games, feeding a Tamagotchi pet and using your parents' old typewriter or solar calculator, you were born to be in the Tech field.

If you are the curious type, likes to know how things work, figures out how to fix things on your own, If you think outside the box and like to do things differently from how most "normal" people would do it, just to see what would happen, you were born to break software.

This might come as a surprise, but most testers are very "Right-Brained" and "Left-Brained." You don't only have to be good at learning things, have a great memory, patience and understand logical stuff, something us moms are already trained for haha, but you must be creative to find defects. Many Testers I have worked with in the past were artists, designers, crafters, or photographers on the side as a hobby. I love to draw, edit photos, write and crochet amigurumi (if you want to see some of my creations, search for <u>AMICREATURES</u> on Etsy).

It's different than being a Developer. You don't need to be good at Math or Programming. People think "Coding" immediately when they think of Computer jobs and feel intimidated and scared, but I suck at Math.

Although now many jobs are asking for "Automation Engineers," which is testers with Developers' skills (or Devs turned testers) who can write scripts, this is just a different branch of testing, one of many specializations in our field.

Don't think you HAVE to be an automation tester to have a great rewarding career as a tester (but of course if you don't mind learning to code, you will open even more doors for job opportunities, the more skills you learn, the better).

A Manual tester can make just as much as an Automation Tester, it's all about diversifying your resume, and I will go over this in the *"Why changing jobs often is NOT a bad thing"* section.

This career is also for you if you get bored easily, if you rather work from home than an office (we have options), if you like change and if you like daily challenges.

Benefits of a Software Testing Career

Here are some benefits of working in this industry.

Variety

You can choose your industry.

Whether you want to work in Medical, Entertainment, Gaming, Gas and Oil, Finance, Government, Space, Aviation, Realty, E-commerce, Streaming Services, etc., there is a job for a tester.

Software is everywhere nowadays; it's not just sitting on a computer. It's in smart cars, smart TVs, kiosks, ad banners, digital posters, watches, toys and everywhere else with a screen, an AI brain or a website. Someone had to test it and pass its Quality Assurance before it hit the market and consumers see it, and that someone could be you.

I think that is my favorite benefit of this career. I can move anywhere I want and find a job because no matter where I go, there will be a company that uses software and needs it to be tested. Whatever your dream company is, they will have and always need QA Testers in their team.

Great Pay

Your salary will increase every year.

Software Testing jobs are very technical and detail-oriented. Although you can get a job without a related college degree (My Bachelor's Degree is in Design), it requires the knowledge of various types of software and various methods of testing (don't worry, we will go over all the different types, so you know which path is best for you).

Again: the more skills you add to your list, the more opportunities and the higher the pay. (I will teach you how to add various testing skills to your resume in the coming chapters.) As an example at the time of writing this book (based on USA salaries) Jr testers at an entry-level position are making $20 to $30 per hour.

Someone with 1-5 years' experience can make anywhere between $30 and $45 per hour as a manual tester, and 5+ yrs experience will put you in the $45-$75 per hour range.

Now, if you learn Automation Testing, which involves programming, you can easily make $70-$120 per hour, even more if you know various programming languages and automation tools. If you specialize in one type of testing and master it, you can easily make six figures a year.

Accessibility testing, for example, pays well over $50 per hour if you have at least 3 years' experience and it doesn't even involve any coding knowledge, although you could add to it and learn HTML and CSS, and now you'd be in the $60 per hour range minimum.

Performance and Load testing alone pay very well too. More about this in the *"How can I earn 6 figures"* section.

Tip: If you are just starting and want to get your foot in the door with little experience, it's easier to start with Video Game testing. They usually hire many first-time testers and just require a high school diploma and some basic computer knowledge. It is the best stepping stone to move on to more complex software later.

Job Security

When was the last time software was replaced by a robot? Never, Software IS the robot!

Now software isn't going anywhere. If anything, it's growing and it's growing at such a fast pace that it's hard to keep up. The world will never have enough Testers. It has been in high demand since I started in 2000 (I started in 1999, but it's easier to count how many years of experience I have if I start counting from an even number, haha).

The day you get laid off or quit a job, it won't take long to find a replacement, especially if you search by your specialized title. That's something not all careers can guarantee. Some careers are specific to location, or industry. We are not. We are everywhere.

The biggest challenge for us as testers is that we can never stop learning to keep up with job security. You need to keep up with the software updates and new programs coming out.

Nowadays, there are competitors for every type of software popping up daily; it's like learning synonyms but with software applications instead of words. Again don't let this intimidate you, if you know one, you can easily learn another one. Most jobs will see the related experience on your resume and be ok with training you on the job.

A good way to keep up with all the Software and have more variety in your resume is to switch jobs often, but we'll get to that later.

Freedom from a specific location

You can work from anywhere!

I don't know if COVID was a blessing in disguise for many in the IT industry, but a lot of companies realized employees could work from home and perform even better, so they kept that option open. For most testing jobs, you can be at home (or the beach if you have Wi-Fi, haha). Working remotely opens a whole lot of new opportunities. You can search for jobs out of state or even out of the country and work from your couch in pajamas.

Few careers give you that comfortable option. Although I am a mother and have 2 full-time jobs from home, I still have to be with my kids and care for everything "household" related.

My husband comes home at 5 pm, and by then, I'm done working my 2 jobs and dinner is ready. I would have never had this opportunity (to get paid for my experience instead of my time) if it wasn't for the pandemic.

Since the pandemic, times have changed and companies realize most employees want to be remote permanently, so many more jobs are offering that option.

If you do miss going to an office occasionally, there are lots of hybrid positions as well, but you limit your search to local companies only.

Should I learn all the types of Testing?

It is absolutely NOT necessary; you can be a "Mobile Tester," an "Accessibility Tester," a "Performance Tester," an "Automation Tester," and many more. All their own category and expertise and all different paying ranges of salaries.

That is something to watch out for when applying for jobs. If a company says they want a "functional tester who also does performance, accessibility, load testing, backend, and API testing as well as mobile," be cautious. They want a jack of all trades and will probably pay the same as a company that just wants an "Accessibility tester."

It's not bad to know more than one type of testing to get a job, and a lot of these titles are the same thing bundled up (you'll see when we go over the different types). Still, some use different technology and software, and you can't be installing it all on one computer. For example, a Performance and Load tester shouldn't also be their automation tester because you will need to install various types of applications for each type of testing, the more you install, the slower the computer will get and give all sorts of problems.

Most companies don't usually require you to perform more than one specialty type of testing, though. During interviews, I usually ask how many testers the team has and what each tester's role is just to clarify what mine will be if hired. I ensure they won't try and burn me out, trying to get me to do more than I can handle.

How can I earn a six-figure salary as a tester?

There are ways for you to increase your salary, so let's go over a few:

Certifications

You don't need a relevant college degree to get a good job as a Tester, but you will need knowledge. How to get knowledge in a short amount of time? Get certified, the more, the better. It takes 2 to 6 months to get certified and with certifications, you can ask for jobs that pay over 100k, especially if you get certified in Accessibility, Performance, and Load Testing, or Mobile App testing.

Remember that usually, the higher rate per hour, the fewer benefits they might offer, and this is ok. You can get your 401k and health benefits on the side if the "recruiters" that hired you don't offer it, although they all usually do after 90 days of employment.

I rather make more per hour than accept a lower-paying salary with all the extra benefits like PTO and paid sick leave, but that's because I'm good at saving and investing on my own, and I'm on my husband's benefits, so it's up to each person to choose what works for them.

Again worth mentioning that if you don't mind learning how to code, getting an Automation certification is a guaranteed 6 figure job.

Another good way to get certified is to wait until you get your first entry-level job and ask about any training or education programs the company offers.

I got all my certifications paid by my employer at my

different jobs. There are many opportunities for employees nowadays that people never take advantage of. Now, if you don't have a job that offers any type of training, I will give resources in the "*How do I get Certified*" section.

Remote Work

Another way is to work remotely. When you go to LinkedIn and search for jobs, type the word Remote after the title. For example: Software Tester Remote. If that doesn't yield results, type Remote in the location. Once the search results show up, that's when the filters appear, and you can select the 'Remote' option from there, delete the word from the Title or Location and Search again (this way, you get results with Remote in the description or somewhere else).

Let's say you find a job that hires you and after a couple of months you figure out your schedule and when you have meetings or need to be online. That's when you can decide if you could handle a second job. For example, I had one job that was remote, but it required a quick turnaround for testing, meaning, the second they sent something to get checked, I had 30 mins to complete the task, so I could never be away from my computer and I had to be on my desk from 8 a.m. - 5 p.m. So even though it was remote, it was hard to have any free time, I quit.

My next remote job had people from different time zones, so we hardly had any meetings, and it was more of a 'work at your own time' schedule, so I would get up at 6 a.m. and by 8 a.m. I was done with my work, we had one meeting and then I was twirling my thumbs the rest of the afternoon waiting for more tasks. I realized I had enough time to get a second job, so I did.

That's when I surpassed my salary expectations by having 2

jobs, it was easier than I expected. None of the meetings overlapped, and if sometimes they did, I would excuse myself from the less important one.

It did not affect my performance at either place. I completed all tasks assigned from both jobs in a timely manner (more on how I did this under the *"Don't be 100% employee"* section). I have lots of friends who have 2 jobs, one has 3. Not in the same industry/career as I did, but at least working from home lets you figure out your schedule and plan something out.

If you have side hustles, the best way to work on those is to get a remote job.

Teaching

Another great way to earn extra cash is to teach on the side. Many apps let you upload a course, so you don't have to teach live, just stream pre-recorded videos or start a YouTube channel.

I have not tried this option yet, but I will be doing it. As I was searching for courses to take myself, I noticed how there were hardly any options. Software Testing is a small niche on high demand.

Freelance

QA testers can offer their services as freelance testers. You choose which jobs to accept and how often. This is a great opportunity to earn more money than the regular 8 - 5 job.

Some good freelance sites are <u>freelancer.com</u>, <u>Upwork.com</u>, <u>uTest.com</u>, <u>Toptal.com</u>, <u>guru.com</u> to name a few. You can sign up and either search for jobs or wait until they find you. <u>Usertesting.com</u> (although this is for anyone, not just QA testers) is a site where you answer short survey questions and if you're a match, they pay $10 per 15 min survey.

It's a good side hustle while you have breaks during your regular job. I usually do about 1 - 2 a day between breaks. That little extra $20 bucks a day can make a difference between having to cook or ordering from Doordash, haha.

Don't be the 100% employee

What does this mean? It means don't give yourself 100% to a job. You are not at a job 24/7, correct? You are there from 8 to 5 or whatever your 8 hr. schedule is, so don't work during lunch, don't skip on breaks to do things, don't answer messages after hours and especially do not work on the weekends. It means take your vacations, take that PTO, resolve urgent family matters and attend school plays if you have PTO saved up. Do not put your job first, family second and yourself third.

You can be at 50% or 60% of your overall potential yet complete 100% of the work. Do not confuse this with being a slacker or doing things half-ass or the bare minimum, I mean the opposite; let me explain:

By giving yourself 100%, you become the 'go-to' person, the one that wants to solve everyone's problems, the one that answers every question in the chat rooms even if not directed at you, the one that responds instantly to emails and chats that are NOT urgent, the person that spends hours trying to figure out someone else's problem while leaving your own tasks on the back burner to solve later, even if it means you must stay over time.

Don't overdo and volunteer to do extra work because you feel guilty if you don't. If you do this, you will never be able to have any free time even when you're at home. Your work-life balance will be off, let alone will you ever have time to have a hobby or a side hustle if you wanted to.

Have you ever been in a relationship where you gave it your all just to be dumped later? Or you broke it off because it felt one-sided, like you were the only one putting in all the effort? Save the best of you for when you think you have found your perfect partner. It's ok to give it your all, if the other person does the same, and you know that will be your future spouse. It's the same thing with jobs, don't overdo unless you are certain that you have found your dream job and you picture yourself retiring from there.

I made this mistake for many years, and it raised expectations. I was expected to do my work, to pick up the slack from others (who earned the same as I did, sometimes more), and even to train the new employees or interns (on top of having to do my required duties) all for the same pay and same title. Of course, you don't need to overwork yourself and do way more than expected to get a promotion or higher position. You just need to do your best during your expected work hours and do it right.

The times I'd be sick, they almost expected me to continue working because I was that person that never let anyone down. If I took time off, I'd feel very guilty, and my co-workers would be a bit lost if they had to complete my duties, especially with the amount of stuff I would complete. I noticed if I took time off, most of the time, my work would just accumulate and wait for me when I went back. No one picked up my slack because I was the person that did that for everyone else. I was becoming everyone's crutch.

When you can help someone, teach them how to do it, do not do it for them; if it's not urgent make them wait until you are free.

People that get favors done instantly get spoiled and will always expect that from you.

Being the 100% employee is NOT a good thing to do to yourself. You are putting yourself in a committed relationship that is not secure because, believe it or not, it does NOT GUARANTEE you will be there when the cuts come.

You will be laid off just like everyone else. When it was my turn, I noticed I was laid off in the last rounds because companies 'keep' their most productive employees until the last minute, but eventually got the boot too, and they were not doing me a favor, it was all for their benefit.

My co-workers who would get laid off first would find the available jobs first, especially back in the day when 'remote' didn't exist, and we all depended on what was around our area.

I have been part of group lay-offs from permanent salaried jobs so often that I finally learned that no job is secure. This is why I always advise accepting any short-term or long-term position (more on this in the *"Why changing jobs often is NOT a bad thing"* section).

I know you may ask, "How will this guarantee me a 6 figure salary?"

Easy, follow this rule: Complete your tasks with "NO EXCUSES."

Never give an excuse for why you couldn't complete a task or finish something on time. Don't be that person with an excuse for everything. I had a co-worker always late to meetings and always had an excuse for why he didn't do something; either his kids, wife, dog or sickness were in the topic. This makes your co-workers not like you as much. It doesn't make them feel sympathy. On the contrary, they also have families and last-minute emergencies, but they still complete their commitments. This might contradict what I said about not putting your family second, but it's one thing to take time off if needed and always complete your work, VS having last-minute excuses, becoming extremely unreliable and not taking deadlines seriously.

You don't need to overwork yourself, but you do need to meet expectations and meet them well. Don't ever have the 'ball in your court' and people waiting on you. This is how you build a good reputation, and good reputations build good bridges and great recommendations for future work. Don't "pencil whip" tasks. A job well done is a job thoroughly tested with a fine comb. Learn to work so well that you trust yourself. Always double or triple-check before submitting results.

Employees with no excuses get raises and trust me when I say 'word of mouth' matters. So when you are done with a job, don't hesitate to ask your co-workers or bosses to leave a good recommendation for you on your LinkedIn profile.

I've worked with hundreds of people but only have a handful of testers and developers with who I would recommend or trust to work again. Exceptional workers are hard to find and guess what; they weren't "100% employees." They just did their job as expected, with no excuses and on time. Ok, with that said, now let's get into the technical stuff.

Most common software and skills that every tester should have as a foundation.

These are what I'd call "general requirements" for a Tester, whatever specialty you focus on (more of that in the "*Types of Testing*" section) there are basic foundations you should know as a QA Tester.

Most common software used in Testing:

- **Basic Computer knowledge:** You need to know the different types of Operating Systems, how to install and use different browsers, how to take screenshots, how to install and uninstall programs, how to access the system settings, display settings, and accessibility settings.

- **Jira**: The most common software used for writing test cases and defects. Jira is also a project management tool that easily integrates with Confluence, Trello and Slack.

- **Confluence:** The most common software used for writing stories and documentation.

- **Trello:** A collaboration tool used for project planning.

- **Microsoft Office Programs:** You will likely use Outlook, Excel, PowerPoint and Word the most.

- **TestRail:** Another common software to write test cases and run them.

- **Snagit**: The most common screen capture tool for screenshots.

- **A chat program:** Zoom, Slack, Skype.

- **Google's cloud services:** sheets, docs, hangouts.

- **Basic SQL:** This is not always required, but I see it more and more in job descriptions, it helps to know the basics.

Most common skills required as a Tester:

- **Good Communication Skills, AKA English**: There is a lot of reading and writing in this career field, part of being a good tester requires you to write detailed test plans and test cases; also writing defects must be concise and clear along with defect reports if needed. You also must read detailed requirements, which can be pages long. That's what "great communication skills" usually means in job descriptions. It's not about being "shy" or "open," it's about how well you communicate with the team, not only verbally but also in written form. As a tester, your English should be proficient in speaking, reading, and writing.

- **Attention to Detail**: If you usually miss small details, you will more than likely miss defects. You need to pay attention to small changes on the program, sometimes, the developers accidentally change the font in one title, or the color isn't the same as the other headers, or a small thumbnail suddenly turned into an error icon. Small details make a big difference. Also, when writing defects, add as many details as you can. It all helps the developers.

- **Great Memory:** Often we are asked, "What version did you find that defect on?" "Do you remember if you tested on all browsers?" "Are you sure that wasn't there before?" "Are you sure it used to behave differently?" Having a good memory can help avoid double or triple checking things.

- **Organized:** If you happen to have a bit of OCD, that's a good thing in this career field. Coming up with a personalized set of rules will make testing much easier. You must have a strategy when it comes to testing, and this is something no one will tell you how to go on about. It's something you come up with. For example, I like to test everything on the homepage first before I click on a link that takes me to another page that has more links that go deeper into the site and end up on a new page. I like to write down everything I test in order. Same thing with Menus that have submenus. You can't just go about clicking everything. You must do it in certain order to cover all ground.

- **Problem Solver:** This doesn't mean you have to fix a defect; you are not the developer. This means you need to make Google your best friend and try and figure things out on your own before asking for help. There's probably a document or YouTube video answering your exact question. There is nothing wrong with asking for help, but that should be your last option since Devs rarely like getting distracted when they are in the coding "Zone." They say it takes an average of 15 minutes to get back into focus, unless you ask a fellow tester, they probably had the same problem you're having, but nothing speaks "self-sufficient" like figuring something out on your own.

- **Be Nice**: I know this seems like a commonsense skill but remember the software you are testing is someone's baby, it's someone's hard work, so be nice when talking to devs about a defect and be nice when re-testing the same thing 5 times.

PART II

What are Software Environments?

When you test something, it's usually in a local environment and not live. If you test a website, let's say *facebook.com*, you are not going to go to *facebook.com* and check there. Most companies have 3 to 6 environments for testing, usually called Staging, Developer, Pre-production and Production. Production is the live site.

An example of a staging URL would be *staging.facebook.com,* where the developers launch their code and want testers to look at it first. Developers usually work on their local environment, which could be called something like *dev.facebook.com* and later, once staging passes QA, they will push to pre-prod, which would look something like *preprod.facebook.com,* and Production being the live *facebook.com* site.

Now, remember these are over-simplified examples. I'm currently working on a staging environment where the URL is as long as the browser window extends haha.

Depending on the size of the company and project, you can have many more environments, my current job for example, has 7 staging environments and like 8 pre-prods. It's not ideal as different developers merge their changes in different environments, causing more merge conflicts, but that is also a lack of unit testing in part of the devs (we'll go over this in the types of testing section).

Most companies stick to 2 to 4 environments for testing.

Sometimes the environments are not on the internet and can't be accessed by simply typing a URL. Sometimes they are local, meaning a local server has the site and to access it, you need to enter the IP address into your host file. Remember to always open Notepad as an Admin or you won't be able to edit the file (on Windows). On Mac, you must be a sudo user to do it via the terminal. You can google how to do this since it's different for MAC and Windows. Sometimes, the environment is only accessed through a virtual machine or remote access.

Every job is different, and they will teach you how to access their different environments and update the different IP addresses.

Test Plans and Test Cases

Test Plan

A Test Plan contains the test strategy, objectives, estimations, deadlines, resources required for completing the assignment, and risks. It's a detailed plan on how the Quality Assurance process will be completed. This is usually done by the QA Manager, lead, or Sr Tester and they usually just type the doc in Word, Confluence, or create it as a PDF.

Note: *For a Test Plan example and Template, visit bettertester.net*

Test Case

A test case is a list of steps that need to be performed to check specific functionality. So whereas the Test Plan encompasses the details of the whole project, a test case is written per section and will just cover a particular scenario.

Test cases usually include:

- Pre-Requisites
- Description of feature or element that will be tested
- Acceptance criteria
- Steps to follow
- Expected results
- Actual results
- Pass/Fail section

Most common software used for writing test cases:

- Word
- Jira

- PractiTest
- TestRail
- TestLink
- TestComplete
- Excel
- Google Spreadsheets

There are many more but again, knowing how to write a test case is the important part, not where to write it. Different companies will use different software, and as long as you get familiar with one or 2 of the above, you'll be fine.

Note: *For a Test Case example and Template go to* *bettertester.net*

How do I write a Defect?

Ok, so a defect is anything that doesn't meet software requirements and anything that's broken or not functioning properly. It could be links that go to a "page does not exist," or to the wrong page altogether, it's images that have the wrong Alt Text, font colors that are different and not consistent with brand standards, grammar errors, menus that don't expand or contract, it's having the wrong total in your shopping cart, etc. You get the idea.

How do you go about writing it?

1. You open the tool the company uses. It could be Jira, Bugzilla, Spira, etc.
2. You perform a search for it first to ensure it's not already written. Nothing worse than having defects marked as "duplicate" clogging the database.
3. You create a new ticket or new defect
4. You make sure to include the following:

- **Clear Title** should contain keywords and be as descriptive as possible in a short sentence. This helps finding defects easier when performing a search (and how we avoid duplicates).

- **Environment** tested on could be staging, dev, pre-prod, production.

- **Operating System** tested on: does it happen on MACs only? Or Windows as well. Is it just on mobile devices? Or desktops too?

- **Browsers** affected: Some defects don't happen on Safari the same as Chrome or IE. Check all the browsers that are supported.

- **Reproducible rate:** is it 100% reproducible? Or does it just happen once in a while, let's say 20% of the time.

- **Short description** is usually a one-liner or short paragraph explaining the defect.

- **Pre-Requisites** is where you list any pre-conditions the user has to have set before performing the test, ex: Have voice over on (if testing accessibility) or have a registered user (if defect involves a profile setting where user is already logged in), have 1000 credits (if test involves redeeming coupons or points for an e-commerce site or gaming site).

- **Steps to Reproduce** is where you write a step-by-step description of how you got to the defect, using a numbered line by line step.

- **Expected Result is** where you write what was supposed to happen.

- **Actual Result** is what is actually happening.

- **Screenshots**, always attach any images or videos that show the defect. Screenshots with nice labels speak volumes.

There will always be other information to fill out that you will learn at the job, for example: the Sprint #, the folder or story it goes into, the team assigned to it, the dev you should assign to, etc.

Most common software used for Defect logging

- **Jira, Bugzilla, Fogbugz, Mantis, HP ALM/QC (Quality Center), BugNET, TFS:** These are all bug/defect tracking tools (or project management tools with defect tracking capabilities), and there are many more, but if you get familiar with one or 2, you have yourself covered for an interview, especially JIRA since that is a project management tool and easily integrates with Confluence, Trello and Slack.

- **SnagIt**: Screen capture tool, easy to use for capturing screenshots. You can always just do a Print Screen on Windows or Shift+Cmd+4 on MAC, but I like Snagit since it lets you add nice editable text labels and arrows.

- **Screen Recorder**: If you want to add a video to your defects, this is easy without any extensions. On Windows 10, press the Windows button + g at the same time. On Mac, press Ctrl+shift+5

Note: For a Defect sample and Bug Template go to betttertester.net

What is the SDLC process?

SDLC Stands for Software Development Life Cycle, the entire process of how a program/game/app or feature/update is done. It doesn't involve just the Testers, but it's important to know since we are part of that process.

The steps have changed over the years. If you google it, you'll see some websites list 7 stages, others 5, others 4, but they all cover the same process.

The different phases more or less are:
- Requirement gathering
- Designing
- Coding
- Testing
- Deployment
- Maintenance

What are the different SDLC methodologies?

Now that you know what SDLC is, there are different types of SDLC methodologies. Below, I will list some of these concepts and a very short description of each (Each one of these methodologies could have its own book.)

- **Agile Model:** This breaks the project into several phases, and the team will perform improvements at every stage. It is the most common methodology and is usually accompanied by SCRUM.

- **What is Scrum?** Scrum is a subset of Agile. The Scrum process enables the company to adjust requirements as they change and evolve. It enables the team to have a smooth project execution through meetings and planning and tackle roadblocks and problems as they come. These are usually done in 2-week sprints.

- **What's a Sprint?** It's the time-box the team must complete one of the abovementioned stages. Breaking a big project into smaller pieces helps the team plan the completion much better. Sprints consist of Sprint Planning, Stand up meetings, Sprint Review and Sprint Retrospective.

- **Waterfall Model:** This model is not used very much but is very simple. It divides the life cycle into a set of phases, but the next phase cannot be started until the first one is completed, so the development process is a sequential flow. One of the drawbacks of this model is that there is no feedback history since it assumes each phase was complete with no errors, and you cannot start the next phase until the previous one is done. Therefore, it's difficult to accommodate any change requests afterward.

- **Iterative Model:** This model starts simple and gets more complex as the development progresses. It's an incremental model.

- **Lean Model:** This model is about working only on what must be worked on. It's all about cutting waste, so dropping unnecessary meetings and documentation.

- **DevOps Model:** This is a newer model that's a mix of Agile and Lean methodologies. Developers and Operations teams work closely together so the deployments are small but frequent.

- **Spiral Model:** This one is similar to the Iterative model. The project passes through the phases (planning, risk analysis, development, and evaluation) over and over in a spiral until it's complete. This is typically used for large projects.

- **V-Model:** In the V-Model the process happens sequentially, parallel to each other. Developers complete something, and testers check it. For example, when they complete Coding and some basic designs, Unit Testing is done, Devs do more high-level design, Integration Testing is done, then they do the Requirements Analysis, so System Testing is performed.

- **Big Bang Model:** This is a model where the team follows no specific process. The development just starts and may or may not meet customer requirements. Little planning is required; even the customer is unsure what he wants, so the process is implemented on the fly. A very simple and easy to manage model gives the team a lot of flexibility, but there is high risk, and it can turn out expensive.

- **RAD (Rapid Application Development) Model:** This model is based on prototyping with no planning involved but after the requirements are gathered. Then the app will go through workshops and focus groups on testing the prototypes. What's nice about this method is that if the customer wants to make changes, the team can rapidly develop and deploy a new prototype. This avoids surprises at the end. The customer who's been involved through the whole process will always get what they want.

- **Prototyping Models:** In this model, a prototype is built, and the customer gives feedback, then the prototype is refined. It is more suitable for high-risk projects compared to the RAD method because the requirements are not clear from the beginning, so it's more fluid and expected to change. The client involvement is high.

Don't get overwhelmed with all this. Most companies use Agile, so get familiar with that one if you must learn one.

What is an SDET?

SDET stands for Software Developer Engineer in Test. It's a new term for Automation Engineers. This is a recent concept since Automation is new, and so are SDETs. This is a developer that helps with QA Testing by writing the necessary scripts to do Automation, or a developer that specializes in QA Testing, or a Tester that learned to code and develop and now specializes in Automation.

What to know to become an SDET?

You need to know everything a manual tester would know and an Automation Engineer as well (details of specific software used will be under *"types of testing"* section). You would need programming skills, plus Agile and DevOps exposure to say the least.

PART III

Types of Testing

Ok, now let's talk about all the different Types of Testing and why just specializing in one area at a time is the best way to become an expert in your field. I'm not recommending just doing ONE type of testing, but learning one at a time. Once you become comfortable with one type, then you can move on to learn another set of skills. Like I said, each type of testing requires its own path of learning, and the more you know, the easier it will be to always be employed.

For example, I work for 2 companies. For one job, I'm an "Accessibility Tester" and for the other company, I do what's called "Creative testing" both are easy to do and require no programming skills, both pay 6 figures a year, and neither requires the full 8 hours for you to be sitting down, I get paid for a full day but finish both jobs after about 4 hours total.

When you work remotely, finding a job that doesn't micromanage you if you get the work done is easy. Most companies usually don't care about what hours you get it done (look for a "flexible schedule" in the job description) as long as you finish your tasks and do them right.

Remember, the longer you work in this field, the more experience you'll gain, and the more experience, the more freedom you'll have, it won't happen overnight, but it won't take a decade either.

Let's dig into some of the different types of testing:

- Creative Testing
- GUI Testing
- Front end Testing

- Functional Testing
- End to End testing
- Responsive Testing
- Exploratory Testing
- Sanity Testing
- Smoke Testing
- Usability Testing
- Regression Testing
- Unit Testing
- Integration Testing
- System Testing
- Acceptance Testing
- Black Box Testing
- White Box Testing
- Gray Box Testing
- Back end Testing
- API (backend) Testing
- Performance Testing
- Load and Stress Testing
- Soak Testing
- Accessibility Testing
- Automated Testing
- Mobile Testing
- Security Testing
- Penetration Testing
- Ethical Hacking
- Risk Assessment
- Vulnerability Scanning

And trust me, there's more I'm not even going to mention because the above are some of the most common ones used among Software Test Engineers (STEs) AKA testers, and what most companies are looking for.

Software is ever revolving and never-ending. It's hard to keep up. Lately, there are many new testing opportunities in Cybersecurity and AI, but they are more fit for developers and programmers than your usual manual tester since you must learn more about software engineering than testing.

Software Engineering (SE) is a different career; sometimes, recruiters mix them up. SEs make the software. STEs break it.

Let's go over each type of testing so you know what they involve. Like I said, you don't need to know them all, but the more skills you add to your resume, the more opportunities open up, and some of these testing types are grouped, so once you learn one, you automatically know 3 or 4 types of software testing.

Creative Testing, GUI Testing, Front End Testing, Functional Testing, End to End testing, Responsive Testing, Exploratory Testing, Sanity Testing, Smoke Testing, Usability Testing, Regression Testing.

Why did I include all these together in the title? Because they are all one group, these tests vary in methodology but have the same backbone with what software is used. You learn one; you learn them all. It's basically what makes a Manual Tester. Sometimes a job will say, "We need a Frontend tester," and not list anything else, but that means you will probably do End to End, Smoke Testing, Exploratory, and everything else listed on the title above.

No worries, after I explain each one, I will add the software used for each testing method.

Creative testing means checking pixels, font, color, image resolution, missing images, borders, padding and margins around buttons, and distance from element to element. It involves checking the design aspect of the website or app.

Most common Software used:

- **Figma**: This is a program used by the UI/UX designers to show the digital images of the website. Nothing is functional. You are seeing the prototype of what the site should look like. This is where you check what font they use, the spacing, measure the buttons size, the padding, margins, exact colors, etc. Everything that concerns graphics, look and brand standards. (Brand standards mean they must use the company's approved colors, fonts and style.)

- **Browser extensions** like **MeasureMate** (Mac), **PixelSnap 2** (Mac), **Dimensions** (Mac), **Caliper App** (Win), **PicPick**. (Windows.) These are used to measure size and distances between elements.

- **Whatfont** is another Chrome extension that tells you the font type, size, color, and more information about a website's text.

- **SnagIt**: Screen capture tool, easy to use for capturing screenshots.

- **Screen Recorder**: To add a video to your defects, this is easy with no extensions. On Windows 10, press the Windows button + g simultaneously. On Mac, press Ctrl+shift+5

Again I am not teaching you HOW to do Creative testing, I could write a whole book on each type of testing, but I am mostly giving you the guidelines on what you need to learn for each type of testing.

GUI (Graphical User Interface) Testing is a mix of Creative and Functional testing. We'll talk more about functional testing below.

Front End Testing involves checking everything the customer would see, what they call GUI (Graphical User Interface) functionality and elements. It checks the "front" of the page. It goes a little bit further than Creative testing because with Front End, you would check it all, including links, button functionality, menu functionality, grammar errors, and anything else you can find wrong with the website or app, unlike Creative testing, checking the "look" more than how it works.

Most common Software used:

- **All the above:** Same as Creative testing but sometimes without the browser extensions. Not all jobs require you to do the "Creative" part of the testing when they require Front End.

- **Jira**: This is the most common Defect Tracking tool on the market. Learn Jira, and you will learn what most companies are using. Jira is used for defect logging and for creating stories (specific features the app/site needs) and requirements.

- **Spira, Bugzilla, FogBugz, Gitlab** are all good bug tracking systems. A quick YouTube video can teach you how to use any of these. Again, you can just learn one, so I'd stick with Jira first as it's the most common.

- **Confluence**: You will see this listed as a job requirement, usually along with Jira. They are both Atlasian products. Confluence is where teams keep their documentation and master stories. It's a project management and collaboration tool.

- **Browserstack**: This is a paid app where you can simulate different browsers, OS systems, and mobile devices. It's used for Cross-browser Testing, which means testing on all browsers.

- **TestRail**: This is a tool where you can write test cases, test plans and run them. It can be integrated with Jira.

- **TestLink**: is another tool for writing test cases, but if you need to know one and know it well, TestRail is much more commonly used.

- **Git and Github:** Git is an Open Source Version Control System. It's something developers install on their computer, while GitHub is a cloud-based platform developers use to upload, download, and share resources.

Now, you don't need to be a developer to learn some simple commands in Git. This is used when multiple developers work in one project. Developers write their code in branches. When they are all done, they merge their code into the "master tree."

Basically, you will open the terminal, and the dev will tell you what command to type to "pull his branch", so when they want you to test a fix or some new feature, you enter the command in the terminal, press enter and voila! You have pulled his branch to your computer, and now you can see their changes in whatever environment they are working on. Again you can learn Git on YouTube, Udemy, Coursera, CodeCademy or atlassian.com/git is also a good one.

Functional Testing, also known as Black Box Testing, is checking that everything already there functions as expected noticing any missing functionality. This is where a tester has a lot of input into the design process and can advise on ways to make it better or implement changes.

Functional Testing is mainly to make sure the application functions as per requirements and meets client expectations. Part of functional testing includes Unit Testing, Sanity Testing,

Smoke Testing, Integration testing, Usability testing, Regression testing, System testing and End to End testing. (We will go over these below.)

See how most of these types of testing involve other types of testing, but they are all part of the same? I know it can get confusing, so the best thing to do is get familiar with all these terms and realize they are mostly synonyms.

Most common Software used:

- All the ones under Front end Testing: **Jira, Confluence, Browserstack, TestRail, TestLink, Git and Github.**

End to End Testing means the same as the 2 above, only you would perform a test in order, a simulation from beginning to end of what a customer would do, for example, if you are testing an e-commerce site and they add a new feature or new functionality to the site and ask you do to do "end to end" test to make sure nothing broke, it means you have to do everything a customer would do the first time they are on the site. For example, sign up, log in, add item to cart, complete order.

This also involves "negative testing," which is doing everything that could go wrong. For example, Forget your password or email, add an item out of stock, use expired credit cards, change qty mid checkout, etc. Again, you tested from one end to the other. Some jobs will list this requirement as E2E.

Most common Software used:

- Same as the ones listed above. As you can see, they are all part of the same testing, just a different name because it's a different approach.

Responsive Testing is the same as Front End testing. Only you resize your browser window to different sizes and see how the website "responds" to this change. All text, images, and links must re-position themselves to fit the window and look good. No overlapping, no weird sizing, and the hotspots (clickable areas) must be where they should be. (Sometimes, the clicking areas move when a window is resized)

This testing involves checking the site or app in different browsers, different operating systems and different mobile devices. One of the easiest ways is checking on Google Chrome. In the developer tools, a mobile simulator will change your browser to different phone screen resolutions.

Most common Software used:

- **Chrome's built-in Developer tools:** To do this using a Chrome browser, simply right click anywhere on the site, select "Inspect," and on the right-side panel (or bottom, depending on how you have your browser set up) click on that little icon on the top left that looks like a phone is in front of a tablet, it's called "Toggle device toolbar" and then on the left side under Dimensions Response there is a drop-down menu with different mobile device models. Choose whichever one you'd like to simulate. It's a good quick way to check for major discrepancies.

This isn't very reliable as a lot of mobile functionality differs from computers. The Operating System is the computer's OS, not the phone's OS, so the functionality is not always the same. It's good for doing quick responsive testing, but if you want to do an in-depth test where it's important that the site works on mobile devices and you don't have access to the "Real" device, then the alternative is to use BrowserStack (windows) or install Xcode (Mac)

- **BrowserStack** (we described above already)

- **Xcode simulator**: This is an app for Mac that can be installed for free through the App Store. Quick explanation on how to use Xcode: Install it, launch it. When the app opens, click on the Xcode menu at the top left (next to the apple icon), click Open Developer Tool> iOS Simulator. This opens an iPhone on your screen, you can close Xcode at this point and the phone simulator will keep running.
  To learn how to change device models on your simulator, YouTube videos teach how to use Xcode pretty in-depth.

- **Screenfly**: simply go to https://bluetree.ai/screenfly/ and you can enter the URL you want to test and see it in different resolutions.

- **CrossBrowserTesting**: this is also a paid app, pretty much BrowserStack's competitor. Does the same thing.

Exploratory testing, as the word says, you are "Exploring" the website. You are clicking randomly everywhere, surfing with no test plan, following no steps. Some of the best defects are found this way, but its part of Frontend Testing and Creative Testing, just out of order.

Usually, when you start a job, your manager will tell you to just do Exploratory testing to get familiar with the site. It's part of training and learning the app.

Sanity Testing is usually done to verify that new functionalities are working properly and not causing new bugs. Sanity testing is a lot like exploratory testing. There are no documents or tests cases to follow. It's very similar to Regression testing (we will talk about this one below), but it only tests one component in the system.

Smoke Testing basically verifies that the critical functionalities of the software are working fine. This covers the most important functions like making sure it launches, that it doesn't crash or freeze, that all images, text and links load correctly.

The tester chooses the most important functionalities and verifies that they are working before they do any extensive testing. It's like turning a car on and verifying none of the dashboard lights are on before taking it for a ride.

Usability Testing focuses on the ease of use of the software, whether it's intuitive and easy to handle.

Regression Testing is like a software checkup after changes or updates have been made to the code. It makes sure the application is still stable and functioning as expected. Regression testing double-checks the new changes haven't broken anything else, it's usually accompanied by Smoke testing and a quick Sanity check.

Most common software used for all the above:

- Same as what's listed under Front End testing.

Unit Testing, Integration Testing, System Testing and Acceptance Testing

Unit Testing is performed on each module, this is usually done by the developers since it tests the code in blocks. It's like a chef that tastes the food as he cooks it and doesn't wait until the final product to discover if he put too much salt. Programmers do the same thing; they test their code in snippets.

Even though it's done by the devs, sometimes QA Testing job descriptions will mention this as a requirement. That's when you know they probably want a dev turned tester or a tester that knows how to code.

You can tell them during the interview that you won't be doing unit tests as it's not a common "tester" task, but:

Most common software used for unit testing:

- **JUnit** if the dev wrote in JAVA
- **NUnit** if it's a .net framework.
- **Jenkins**: which provides a host of plug-ins for unit testing in JUnit.

Integration Testing checks the software after all these said "units" have been merged into the rest of the code. One piece of code can contain various modules and be made by different developers, so integration testing is very important to make sure "they all get along" and break nothing. A tester can check all the modules individually and make sure they all work as required.

For this type of testing, you check the front end, so the software used is the same as what's listed under Front End testing.

System testing falls under Black Box testing (no worries, we'll go over that as well) it checks the "System" as the name says. This means you test based on the requirements. For example, if it says it works on Windows 8 and above, you test on Windows 8 and above.

It also involves checking external peripherals with it. Believe it or not back when I was a video game tester, sometimes, the games would freeze when you switched controllers or changed the keyboard or mouse, so hardware testing is part of this.

All these components and combinations of components are part of the System, same with memory issues and slow processors. The software needs to function per the documents in the system requirements. System testing is more of a synonym for doing Functionality, End to End, Performance and Usability testing.

Most common Software used:

- Besides those listed under Front End testing, you will sometimes be required to install a Virtual Machine. For example, if you have a Mac, you might need to test a Windows system. You might need to install a Virtual machine with an older version of Windows and a different set of browsers and versions if you have a Windows.

Acceptance Testing is done by UAT Testers or Beta users. You might be asked to do this at your job. By now, the software should be ready for the client. UAT means User Acceptance Testing, and it lets users check a beta version of the software or website right before launch. Beta users act like real users and will basically do a full Front End Testing, usually in the way of an E2E or Exploratory testing.

Most common Software used:

- Since these are usually done by outside users or the client checking the app, the basic software used is mostly screen capture apps like Snagit, for them to add to their defects and sometimes they enter their defects directly into whatever software is used by the company, whether it's Jira or Spira, Bugzilla, etc. Most of the time these users just enter their defects into Word, Excel or Google Spreadsheets and email it to their superior for them to later do what's called a "Triage" with the QA team.

Quick explanation of Triage:

This is where the company's QA team and the UAT team (usually just the managers, not the UAT testers) go through all the defects together and determine whether it's one of the following:

- **Duplicate**: *A defect* already written by a tester that just hasn't gotten fixed yet or needs to be re-opened.
- **Change of Order:** Something not listed in the Requirements from the beginning which the client can then proceed with fixing it (which will be an additional cost) or just leave as is.
- **New valid defect**: Something the testers missed that should be logged.
- **Invalid Defect or NAB** (*Not a bug):* When the defect is per design or a feature the client wasn't aware of.

During this Triage period, they will also prioritize the defects into severity and what needs to be done first or not.

White Box, Black Box and Gray Box Testing

Ok, so you might have heard these terms before and wondered the differences, here's a quick breakdown of what each entails, and again you need not be proficient in them all. I personally just do Black box testing.

White Box Testing is for testers that understand code. It lets the tester look at the internal part of the software and checks things like code structure, branches, loops, conditions, etc. It's something performed more by developers than testers. The software used is probably the same as what's used for Unit Testing.

Black Box Testing does not require you to know programming and it's very similar to System Testing and Acceptance Testing. However, you primarily concentrate on functionality and base it on the requirements.

Gray Box Testing is just a new label they gave to someone that does a combination of White Box and Black Box Testing.

Can you see a trend now and how so many of these types of testing are basically the same thing broken into different methods and fancy names? As a tester as long as you make sure it all works as expected, you have pretty much covered all the above types of testing (the ones that do not need programming skills, that is).

API Testing, Performance Testing, Load Testing, Stress Testing, Soak Testing

API (Application Programming Interface) Testing falls under the Performance Testing categories. API testing checks for functionality, performance, reliability and security, requiring the tester to communicate with the API (Backend).

When someone says they want you to do API testing, you will want to do Performance, Load, Stress and Soak Testing. API is Backend Testing, so testers that perform API tests will also do White Box Testing and, most of the time, know how to code, which means they can also do Automation Testing if they learn how to use the automation apps. See how based on your skills, we can group types of tests?

An API or Performance tester can be a specialty, meaning you can become a "Performance Tester" and make a great salary, so let's dig in below:

Performance Testing is identifying the breaking point of the application. You are testing the software stability under a particular workload.

You test:

- **Speed and Memory**: How fast the application responds and what working storage space is available.
- **Scalability**: What's the maximum user load it can handle.
- **Stability**: How stable is the software under different loads.

Load Testing, Stress Testing and Soak Testing are Types of Performance Testing.

Load Testing is where the tester will simulate the expected number of users on the application to see if it can handle it and find out how long it takes to respond. It finds bottlenecks in the system.

Stress Testing purposely places the system under much higher traffic loads to see the expected capacity limits. Usually, companies perform these tests when they expect higher than usual traffic, like ticket sales for an anticipated concert event or Black Friday sale.

Stress testing has 2 categories Soak Testing and Spike Testing.

Soak Testing is leaving the system on/running overnight. It tests how the system runs over a long period of time; it can be anywhere from 6 hours to 24 hours.

They also use this type of testing for websites that have user accounts to check that a logged-in user gets logged out after a certain period, to test the correct warning modals pop up, to test idle mode, and make sure the system goes to sleep if it's supposed to go to sleep, to check correct time outs.

I'll never forget the day one of my co-workers was sleeping on the job, and when my boss kicked his chair to wake him, he responded, "What boss? I'm soak testing." And went back to sleep hahah.

Most common Software used:

- **JMeter**: or Apache JMeter, this is a Java-based open-source software used to do performance and load testing. This is the most common one used, so if you want to start by learning one app, learn this one.

- **SoapUI:** This is used for SOAP API and REST API testing. I won't go into these subtypes of API Testing, but if a job requires Soap or Rest API testing, then you know you need to learn SoapUI.

- **Postman:** is an application also used for API testing. It tests HTTP requests.

- **LoadRunner:** is a good tool used for checking the system under load. This is used for Load Testing, it's like JMeter, only it's not free, and it's made by HP instead of Apache. You can learn them both to maximize your opportunities at a job interview or as I said before, jobs list all synonyms. You can just learn JMeter to begin with.

- **LoadUI:** This is another free open-source tool also used for Load Testing. Checks web services' speed and scalability by allowing you to simply drag different components around.

- **Apache:** this is a web server that runs 67% of all websites in the world, it's a free open-source software. If you will be doing API testing, you need to get familiar with Apache WebServer.

- **Appvance:** This is an automated AI-driven continuous

testing system, used for functional, performance and security testing.

- **WebLOAD:** This is another tool used for performance, stress and load testing.

Accessibility Testing

This is another type of testing that's a whole specialty on its own, you can become an Accessibility Tester (and yes, get certified) as a career, and it pays very well.

Accessibility also known as A11y (why did someone name it that? Because there are 11 letters between A and Y, clever, I know).

This type of testing aims to ensure the application meets ADA (Americans with Disabilities Act) Standards. It's making sure the website, game, application or whatever you are testing is accessible to people with disabilities, and that doesn't mean just people visually impaired or hearing impaired. That can be anyone who has trouble in some area of their cognitive abilities, even if temporary for example, a person who just had surgery and can't use the mouse well, someone that's color blind, someone that needs hearing aids, an elderly person who simply can't read small font or someone that had eye surgery.

Websites can get sued if they do not meet accessibility requirements, also called 508, W3C, ADA and WCAG, which is why this testing has gained popularity and why Accessibility Testers are in high demand with jobs often paying 6 figure salaries, plus can be done remotely.

Things to learn to become an Accessibility Expert

First, you need to learn the WCAG (Web Content Accessibility Guidelines.) The most current one being WCAG 2.2, but 3.0 is coming out soon. This is a set of rules, a checklist per say that applications need to meet to pass A11y requirements.

There are 3 levels of compliance in WCAG: A, AA, and AAA. These are levels of criteria that must be met: A means meeting minimum compliance, AA being Acceptable compliance, and AAA being Optimal compliance. You can learn about WCAG at w3.org and w3c.GitHub.io/WCAG/requirements/22/

One of my favorite checklists is at WCAG-filter-tool.netlify.app. Although it's the WCAG 2.1 standards, not much has changed and it's still very useful and relevant.

Now, you also need to learn how to use specific tools associated with accessibility. The most important being "Voice readers," "Scanners," and "Screen Magnifiers."

Voice Readers

Voice Readers read everything you do on the computer out loud. It will let the user know what is selected. Whether it's a button, a link, a tab, an expanded menu, you get the idea. It will tell the user the type of element he has highlighted. It will read headers, image descriptions and the main text.

These are called "ARIA" labels, also known as WAI ARIA. These are labels hidden in the code, for example, when a user expands a menu, you read nowhere on the site "expanded menu" because you can just see it. A person with visual impairments needs to know it's open, so the aria label, which is written in the code, needs to have an "expanded menu" label for the Voice Reader to say it out loud. Get it?

It's not very complex to spot areas that need ARIA labels. Now, if you'd like to tell the developer exactly where the label is missing and suggest a fix, you need to learn HTML, CSS and JavaScript as well.

For Windows, we use JAWS or NVDA, which are apps you must install, and for MAC, you can use VoiceOver, which is easily activated in the settings, no need to install anything (press the power button 3 times on MacBook Pros).

Scanners

Now we also need to learn how to use Scanners; these are browser extensions that are easily found by doing a google search for "Accessibility scanners."

Scanners do what the name says, "scan" the website, and then give you a list of errors based on WCAG standards it thinks it didn't meet. I say "thinks" because sometimes the developers will let errors go if they are not that severe or by design.

Some of the most common errors include color contrast, images being labeled incorrectly or not labeled, links not informing the user where the URL will redirect to, elements not properly labeled, ARIA labels missing (and yes, the scanner will highlight the section on the site to which the error is referencing).

Most common scanners used for desktop:

- Axe
- Lighthouse
- SiteImprove
- Wave

Magnifiers

These are used to see the screen as if we were using a magnifying glass. It makes the icons, text and images much bigger. It's like using a temporary zoom function. You can activate it on Windows 10 and higher by pressing the WIN button and the Plus (+) button and tapping the plus until you get the desired size, or by pressing CTRL + ALT + Mouse scroll, or by simply opening the Search from the taskbar and typing "magnifier." Press WIN + ESC to get out of it.

On Mac, go to System Preferences > Accessibility > Zoom > and from there, you can select how you want the screen to zoom in.

Accessibility Testing on mobile

- **Accessibility Scanner (Android)**, once installed, go to settings > installed services > accessibility scanner > and allow permissions 'on.' Now you can just go back to your website or app on your mobile and test it. You'll see an orange box around potential accessibility issues.

- **TalkBack (Android)**: Go to Settings > Accessibility > TalkBack > and tab it on. Using this, the user can interact with their device without seeing the screen and check for any errors.

There are two ways to navigate your applications using TalkBack:

- Linear Navigation
- Explore by touch

- **VoiceOver (iOS)**: Go to Settings > General > Accessibility > VoiceOver and tap the switch control to turn VoiceOver on. Check to make sure the Speak Hints switch is on, in case the devs created speaking hints for any accessible element.

You can also turn on VoiceOver using the triple-click Home button setting (click Home button 3 times) but you must set it up first by going to Settings > General > Accessibility > Triple-Click and then select which A11y function you want to assign to it.

Hardware used for Accessibility testing

Some assistive devices for Accessibility testing include special keyboards and mice, mouth sticks, head wands, button switches, sip and puff switches and braille display. Usually, as a tester, you won't be getting these for testing. Instead, you will more than likely test with your regular keyboard/laptop and mouse/touchscreen using the scanners and voice readers.

There is a lot you can learn if you just focus on Accessibility testing, and this is a great career to specialize in this field. I just wanted to give you a quick look at how some of the A11y testing is set up, but now that you know what you need to learn, it's up to you learn it in depth.

You can become certified in different types of accessibility testing. I will list the URLs under the "How do I get certified section."

Automated Testing

This is another type of testing you can specialize in and very high in demand. So automated testing is checking the software with scripts. It still must validate that the software is working correctly and meets all requirements, only this time, you tell the computer how to do it for you.

You can do all the testing mentioned above with automation. The process is simple:

First, you choose a tool, then you define the scope of what will be tested, then you'll plan how to go about it, develop it (write the code), execute it (run it) and check the results. You also need to maintain it meaning make changes and update the code as the software/website changes.

Most common software used:

- **Selenium WebDriver:** This is the most popular automation tool on the list. It is both a functional and performance automation tool. It automates browsers, so it's mostly used for web testing; it does not support desktop or mobile applications. It supports Chrome, Firefox, Opera, Safari and IE. It supports various programming languages, the most common being JAVA, Python, PHP, Perl, Ruby and C#.

To run Selenium scripts, you need to install an IDE (Integrated Development Environment); an IDE lets you edit the source code, build executables, and debug. It also provides visual cues, keywords with special meaning, highlight a different color, and it has autocomplete.

Here's a list of some of the best IDEs to run Selenium using JAVA:

- Eclipse

- IntelliJ IDEA

- NetBeans

You will hear people arguing over which one of these is better, most testers prefer either Eclipse or IntelliJ over NetBeans. I liked Eclipse. When I installed NetBeans, my computer ran slow.

Best IDEs to run Selenium using Python:

- **PyCharm:** Compatible with Linux, Mac and Windows, its one of the better IDEs in Python.

- **PyDev:** If you develop in Python and like Eclipse, you can install a Plug-in called PyDev.

- **Cucumber:** Cucumber supports BDD (Behavior Driven Development) and it's used writing in Gherkin language (*Given, When, Then* format). It's mostly used for writing the user stories. It is not a Framework like Selenium. It's more of a testing tool used to write readable scripts but runs these scripts slowly. It's used for story testing, whereas Selenium is used for API, UI, functional, frontend testing. Again both only support web applications.

- **Cypress:** is a selenium alternative. It allows devs or testers to create scripts using JavaScript.

- **Eggplant:** is also a Functional testing tool used for automation and debugging.

- **UFT -** formerly known as QuickTest Professional (QTP) Unified Functional Testing can provide functional and regression testing using automation for desktop and web-based applications.

- **HP ALM - formerly known as Quality Center (QC):** This is a very common Project Management tool, very similar to Jira (more expensive though, so more companies are switching to Jira and buying the Add-ons to make it as complete as HP ALM for SDLC). HP ALM is mostly used by companies that haven't upgraded their tech (government agencies anyone?). It only supports old versions of IE and windows, which is why it's losing popularity compared to JIRA. So why am I including it in the list of Automation tools? Because you will need to install HP ALM to run tests with UFT and LoadRunner.

Mobile Testing

Mobile testing is also a specialty on its own. You can become a mobile tester and be always in high demand. This is one of those careers that is growing daily.

Mobile Testing can be separated into 2 categories: Manual and Automated. I've tested websites on mobile, but that was more related to "responsive testing" since I was just checking the website on a browser on a mobile device. I'm a manual tester, so I perform all the same types of tests as I do on desktop (Frontend, End to End, Smoke test, Creative, Exploratory, etc.) So for manual mobile testing, you would have to learn all the manual testing techniques just the same. What you must add to your list are the software tools specific to mobile testing.

If you want to do Automation Mobile Testing, you will have to learn everything an Automation Tester would learn, and then add to that list the apps used for automation mobile testing specifically.

For all Mobile testing, you need to learn:

- iOS App Testing
- Android App Testing
- Cloud-Based Mobile App testing service providers

Most common applications used for Mobile Testing:

- **Appium**: This is most widely used for functional testing; it does *native, mobile and web automation*. To specialize in Mobile testing this is the one I'd learn first. (Android and iOS)

- **TestComplete** does automation for UI tests (Android and iOS)

- **HeadSpin**: does manual and automated tests (Android and iOS)

- **Avo Assure:** this is a no-code automation tool (Android and iOS)

- **Katalon Studio:** This is the leading Appium alternative. Does automated tests, no programming background needed (Android and iOS)

- **Eggplant:** used for functional, creative, cross-browser and automated testing (Android and iOS)

- **Test IO:** for manual cross-browser and cross-device testing (Android and iOS)

- **UI Automator:** for automated functional test cases (Android)

- **Ranorex:** code-less click and go interface for automated testing (Android and iOS)

- **Selendroid:** this framework lets you simultaneously interact with multiple devices and emulators. This is an automated tool, selenium for Android.

- **UFT Mobile**: used for automation, can test on mobile devices or emulators (Android and iOS)

- **Robotium:** code-less automation for black box, UI, function, system and user acceptance testing (Android)

There are many more apps for mobile testing, but if you learn just one or a few, then you have put your foot through the door. If you choose this path as your specialty in testing, there are great resources to get started. Please see my *"Resources"* section for more information.

You can also get certified as a Mobile Tester (more in the *"How do I get Certified"* section) and you can also get certified by learning how to test on a specific app, for example, <u>edureka.co</u> offers a *"Mobile App Testing using Appium"* course, which upon completion gives you a **"Mobile App Tester Certificate."**

Most common apps used for Performance and Security testing on Mobile:

- Blazemeter
- ImmuniWeb
- Zed Attack Proxy
- Quark
- Micro Focus
- Android Debug Bridge
- CodifiedSecurity
- Synopsys
- MobSF (Mobile Security Framework)

Security Testing, Penetration Testing, Ethical Hacking, Risk Assessment, Vulnerability Scanning.

All the above are part of Security Testing, which is also a career on its own. You can become a Security Tester as well as get certified in the fields separately. For example, get an Ethical hacking cert, or a Penetration Testing certification, etc. This type of testing is done to check for weaknesses in the application and guard against hackers or intruders. Many industry regulations require organizations to perform regular security testing, so when you see some jobs asking for ISO 27001, PCI, DSS or SOC2, that's what they are referring to. They want a Security Tester.

There are a lot of types of security testing so let's go over a few below:

Penetration Testing simulates a cyber-attack against the application, network or system under secure conditions. It must be done by a certified security expert to measure the strength of its security. They also call this Pen-Testing.

Ethical Hacking goes a bit deeper than Pen-Testing and it includes its own sub-hacking methodologies. These tests try all misconfigurations and check all vulnerabilities by simulating attacks from within the software app.

Risk Assessment involves an analysis of the security risks, which can be low, medium or high. This type of testing would recommend how to reduce the risk.

Vulnerability Scanning is done with automated software to scan vulnerability patterns in the application.

There is also **Posture Assessment**, a mix of Ethical hacking, Risk Assessment and Security/Vulnerability Scanning.

Some examples of Security testing can include:

- Passwords that must be encrypted when stored
- Authentication so fake accounts and invalid users are not allowed to access the application
- Certain cookies should be checked
- Going Back on a browser should not work on financial websites
- Data integrity
- Security Authorizations
- Confidential material
- Network and Server security

Now for this type of testing, I can't just list the software used because there are different categories of tools depending on what type of testing we're doing. These are SAST, DAST, IAST, SCA and RASP.

SAST (Static Application Security Testing) these tools assess the source code while at rest and it's usually done before the app is live and running. This can be done with White Box testing.

DAST (Dynamic Application Security Testing) examines the application while it's running. These types of tools use a wide range of attacks to try and detect conditions on which the application can be exploited. Black box testing is used for this, and it doesn't have access to the source code.

IAST (Interactive Application Security Testing) tools

combine both Static and Dynamic testing and try out various techniques to simulate advanced attack scenarios.

SCA (Software Composition Analysis) tools are used to track open source components.

RASP (Runtime Application Self Protection) this tool is different than the ones above because it's used after product release. It's a technology that intercepts calls from the app to the system, ensuring they're secure.

PART IV

Is Manual Testing being replaced by Automation testing?

No, it is not. As a manual tester, seeing all these new job postings listing "automation" in the requirements can feel scary.

It is becoming popular, but you will never be able to replace a manual tester; In fact, many companies will list "automation" as either a "bonus" or "nice to have," but it's not usually mandatory if it is, then they should've listed "automation" in the job title as it can be its own specialty.

Doing Automation testing is writing scripts to run your "manual" tests faster. It's a tool, but a tool cannot work without an expert. A person that just knows how to code and write scripts cannot be an Automated tester because he has no testing experience and wouldn't know what to tell the scripts to look for, but a manual tester can use automation as an extra tool to help them test faster.

Companies don't always expect a Frontend tester or an Accessibility tester to know automation, but they can hope they find one. Now, if you do learn automation, you will open a lot more opportunities for yourself because the company will see it as "killing 2 birds with one stone," and they won't have to hire another tester that specializes in Automation or an SDET and you will get a higher salary.

But don't let this intimidate you. There are still plenty of jobs out there for manual testers. Automation is an extra skill added to the manual testing process, not a job killer.

Why Job Descriptions list so many requirements not required

If you've ever looked on Facebook Marketplace or Craigslist, you will notice that the best way to find more matches is to use more keywords. I know they usually say, "Narrow your search" to get better results, which is true if you want something very specific, but if you just need a "dining table" and you don't care what color, then you'll just search for dining table, not "white oval glass 6 seater table."

It's the same with job ads. Most recruiters want as many candidates as possible to apply and weed out the less qualified ones. So, for example, you see a job that says "familiarity with Jira, Fogbugz, HP ALM/QC" it doesn't mean they want you to know all those programs, but they would consider a candidate that knows at least 1. If you know 2, great. If you know 3, excellent, but they won't expect you to know them all.

Don't be afraid to apply for a job you think you are not qualified for just because you don't meet all the requirements listed. If you meet about 30%, you have a good chance of getting an interview. To this day, I have never met 100% of the requirements in a job description.

Best way to find a job and have recruiters find me

The best way to find a job is to have your LinkedIn profile up to date. I have used all job search engines, and most of the job's I've gotten were thanks to LinkedIn.

I'm sure by now you've heard of **monster.com**, **indeed.com**, **careerbuilder.com**, **creativecircle.com**, **ziprecruiter.com**, etc. All great for finding job ads BUT rarely do they reply to you after you've applied through their platform. It's like recruiters ignore applications coming from those sources, so what I do is I see job openings on those sites, then search for that specific company on LinkedIn, go to their landing page, click on the JOBS tab and then search for that specific job. Often, you will see it's not even listed. That's because LinkedIn has the most up-to-date jobs and openings, while Monster and other sites keep job postings listed long after closing.

Or you can search directly on LinkedIn under their Jobs section. In short, the best way to find a job is through LinkedIn.

After updating your profile, adding all the skills you know, adding certifications, if any (with photos), getting recommendations (ask old co-workers to write a recommendation for you, more than likely, they will do it). You have only to set your profile to OPEN FOR WORK.

You do this by going to your profile page on LinkedIn. Under your header/title, there are 3 buttons, click on "Open to," select "Finding a new job," and then you can select some nice options like whether you want it on-site, hybrid, or remote. The best part is you can enter various job titles so you can type general ones like "Software QA Tester" or be very specific like "Accessibility

Tester" or both. Then just watch your inbox flood with requests. I have found this to be the most useful tool for employers and employees to connect about job opportunities.

Also, since it's a networking website, you can add those recruiters to your contacts whenever they have other openings.

Feel free to add me to your contacts, my LinkedIn profile is **https://www.linkedin.com/in/jennifer-barbour-qa** or follow me on Twitter @bettertester1 or Instagram @bettertesterqa I'll try and post useful stuff occasionally.

Why changing jobs often is NOT a bad thing

Ok, so we've all been told about job loyalty and how staying in one place for a long time shows we're reliable and secure and how we need to commit to a job as if it was a marriage, how pensions, 401k's, and benefits are the biggest reason to stay put.

It's all BS with Tech jobs. Unless you have found your dream company, the one you've wanted to work at for years, the one you envisioned yourself retiring from, and the one that makes you proud and smile ear to ear when you see their logo, then it's ok because being happy is more important than getting that raise. Still, if you are like the other 90% of Testers who work wherever they can, you don't need to feel the "guilt" when moving around.

First, let me start by saying the average company salary increase is 3-7% per year, while the average rise in salary you get by switching jobs is 12-20%, you can google it if you don't believe me. (I saw the article on LinkedIn.)

Here's my personal experience so I can attest that the study is true:

Since the end of 2019, I've had 4 jobs. One was a salary position, and the other 3 were contracts. I've had an hourly increase of about $5 per hr. per job. So I increased my hourly rate $20 dollars in 4 years. Had I stayed in my job from 2019, I would probably have increased $5 per hour, so a little over a dollar per year.

Calculating my exact earnings, I had a 48.6% increase in salary in 4 years by switching jobs, which comes up to 12.15% increase per year. (That is almost scary how accurate that study was about your salary increase is at least 12%.) Why do you think that happens? Because being a Software Tester is a high-demand technical job. You are not doing yourself a favor by staying loyal to one place when thousands of openings and companies are willing to fight for top talent.

Also, most contracting agencies do offer benefits, 401k and some sick leave after 90 days on the job.

There are way too many software apps, techniques, and skills out there used for QA Testing. It would be impossible for you to gain experience in various of those apps by staying at the same company.

Whether you get a permanent position, 12-month contract, 6-month contract or 3-month contract offer, accept it. What you want is the experience and to add to that list of skills, which in turn makes it much easier to find the next job and the next, so even though you might feel like you don't have that "job security" from a permanent position, you are more secure than people that stay in one place for a decade.

You'll see when you hit that "I'm open for work" button on LinkedIn, all these recruiters will see your list of skills and want you in their team. If you find a job that offers a 6+ month contract with a chance to turn permanent, take it, and if you like it, accept the offer to become a permanent employee, but at 2 years max, you should be looking for a new job and in the next interview when they ask you why you left your last position, simply say "They had no more room for growth," recruiters love candidates that want to grow in their field.

I love short-term contracts because it allows me to see if I like working in that industry, be it gaming, gas and oil, healthcare, etc. If I hate the job, I just wait it out until the contract ends and kindly decline if they offer to extend it. No guilt of quitting when you're a contractor, plus you get to learn what type of testing you love to do most.

I love testing in the gaming industry, e-commerce and streaming apps the most. I learned I don't like banking, government agencies or healthcare. I would have never learned that had I stayed at those jobs permanently. You get to learn more about your preferred style of testing by moving around.

I now know I prefer Accessibility Testing over any test that requires SQL or excel spreadsheets. Although I know automation, I didn't like it, so I'm sticking to more manual testing. Some of my old co-workers discovered they are very good at Performance testing and others at Automating, so they specialized in those fields. One of my old co-workers loved security testing instead, so now he does that. We all met during our video game testing years.

Only by switching jobs and trying different types of testing can you choose your specialty much easier and focus on that for the future.

How do I write my Resume?

One of the biggest mistakes people make when writing their resume is in their BIO section. They make it too long, you don't need an intro section that is more than one short paragraph, and that's if you want one. I, for example, don't have a bio or any introduction in my doc Resume (the word version I send recruiters) but I do have a small bio in my online resume and on my LinkedIn profile.

My resume is 5 pages long (with 12 jobs and around 15 references listed). A resume with a lot less experience should not be over 2-3 pages max. Don't add fluff.

Also If you take a break for maternity leave, just list it there, I made the mistake once to call that break "personal time off to work on projects" like writing this book, but that turned off recruiters, they thought it was a fancy way of saying "not hirable" haha, and advised me to just list it as "parenting full time" or "maternity leave"

After listing your experience, education and certifications you can add extra skills non-QA related like for example hobbies, side gigs, interests. Don't add your biography or where you come from. They don't care, all they want to see are keywords. Do you know the software they require? Do you have the skills making a test plan, writing defects? What job duties did you perform at each position? That's all they care about.

Note: *For a Resume template and more, please visit betttertester.net*

How do I nail an interview?

Now, this is one of the questions I get emailed all the time, but it's difficult to answer. Sometimes you meet all the skills they want, yet you are out of their pay range, or let's say you have relevant experience, not the exact type of software they want. (For example, you know JIRA, but they use Bugzilla), so they might consider you based on years of experience or how easy you'll be to train. Remember, most companies hire based on potential. The downside is you never know who else they are interviewing. Maybe they happen to get lucky and find someone that meets most of their requirements and happens to have more years of experience, then you can only hope they won't accept the salary offer.

But here are my basic tips for getting that second interview and potentially that job offer:

- **"So let's talk a little bit about yourself"** this is the most common sentence you'll hear during an interview, do not go into where you were born, how you were raised, how many siblings you got, and how you were the best in your math class (or the worst haha). Don't go into your hobbies and your favorite foods.

  What they mean is, *"Tell me what kind of a tester you are and why we should WANT you"* I always start with "Well, I started by working at Mattel testing Barbie games," and then I go into my next job and my next one and when I mention each job, I explain how my duties changed, for example, "When I started at DirecTV I no longer tested just frontend, but also hardware and API on the cable boxes."

- **Interviewers LOVE keywords**. That's what they write down. You must mention your duties at each job and the software that was used but do it in one short sentence, "at this place, I managed 2 interns, wrote the test plans and I designed the defect report template since they had an outdated one, we used Jira and Confluence."

- **Then tell them why you left.** Some of my reasons included "Then I left this place because I moved out of state" or "Then I left when the contract ended and started at this other place," "There was no room for growth. They had no higher positions than where I was at" or my latest "Then COVID happened and my job cut my hours... or didn't offer remote work... or we all got laid off as a group." All the above have been true reasons.

Never tell them you quit because you hated the job, or simply got bored and wanted change. You don't want them to think you are unstable. Remember, whenever you do get a job, be the best you can be even if you plan on quitting in a couple of years, never burn bridges no matter how much you want to vent. Always think about your reputation.
I usually get through that "tell me about yourself" question in less than 3 minutes.

- **Make them WANT you.** Be confident but not arrogant. Talk about your skills, how you think you can be a great asset for the company, and how you read the job description and it was right up your alley. Let them know the job description sounded like they were describing you. Read about the company before an interview. It looks good when you tell them why you would love to work for them specifically.

Tell them you like testing that software and, most importantly, tell them how you are eager to learn, you are a self-starter who learns things fast, and you can't wait to add their name to your resume. Even better if you have had experience and you can tell them, "This sounds a lot like what I did for such and such company." Real life examples and experiences are the most memorable for the interviewer.

When you show you are excited and would be proud to be a part of their company, not just excited about the job itself, they will consider you even if you are not an exact match for that position, they might need a junior tester or another type of role than the one you applied for, and they will remember you for future openings.

- **When they ask, "What has been your biggest challenge,"** make sure it's a technical answer, they don't mean in life. Don't say, "Raising 3 kids while working from home." Haha, they mean during a job.

My biggest challenge, for example, has always been setting up the environment. I tell them I'm not a developer and sometimes installing certain software has been very technical and out of my scope of expertise.

Another challenge has been working with testers that

liked to "pencil whip" and weren't very reliable because when they missed things, and obvious defects got through, we all looked bad as a QA team, not just the individual.

I have also shared how sometimes it's a challenge to approve things that aren't very user friendly because, obviously, as a tester, you want everything perfect and pretty, but if it's out of scope and something the client didn't pay for, then we must stick to the simple requests and requirements.

Another challenge we face as testers is getting the build on time. If working in sprints and the team has 2 weeks to complete a phase, guess how long the developers usually take making it? 2 weeks! They don't always consider testing time or worse, time to fix all the defects.

Overconfident developers could be the single biggest challenge for a tester. You need at least 3 days to test before that last Friday to make sure they fix the defects, and you do regression testing.

How do I get Certified?

Different types of Certifications and where to get them:

A lot of the places I'll list below offer multiple types of certifications in various specialties, but I'm breaking them down by specialty for easier reference.

For Manual, Automated and many other types of testing:

- **ASTQB:** Go to astqb.org/certifications/ and on the right side you will see all the specialties you can get certified on. The most common one being the ***ISTQB Foundation Level Software Testing Certification (CTFL)***. After you get the foundation cert, you can apply to get the more advanced ones.

- **QAI:** Go to https://www.qaiglobalinstitute.com/software-certifications-2/ and scroll down. You will see a list of their software tester certificates you can get based on their courses. So the reason I'm giving you this site is that it's a good place to get the training needed, and it has all the links to the places that provide the certification. The most common one or the best one to start would be the ***CAST certificate (Certified Associate in Software Testing)***; you can click that link from the URL above OR you can go directly to their site software **certifications.org/cast** and get it if you are already

ready for the test.

- **GAQM**: Go to gaqm.org/certification/software_testing and you will see a list of the certifications they offer along with the learning path.

Automation Tester:

Here are a few good sites to get trained and certified in Automation testing:

- **Simplilearn**: Go to simplilearn.com and type Automation Test Engineer in the search engine. Click on their top result, "***Automation Testing Master's Program***." This course will give you good automation training, it's not just basics or using one app. Most of the common ones like Maven, TestNG, Selenium, Docker, and Appium, you will learn Core Java and how to automate web apps. This course will make you an expert.

- **Edureka**: edureka.co great to learn one app at a time, based in India. I took a Selenium Certification course there and it was good. I'll probably take the Appium class next. Again their certifications aren't as known as other reputable places, but lots of knowledge at an affordable price.

- **LambdaTest**: lambdatest.com/certifications/ is a good place to learn Selenium (with various programming language options), Cypress, JUnit, TestNG and get certified.

- **Udemy**: If you go to udemy.com you can learn anything you want related to testing, BUT the certifications of completion aren't as accredited as the ones from ISTQB per se. There are usually no tests or assignments, so when the videos are completed watching, you will get a little PDF automatically generated saying you finished the course. Great affordable learning app, though.

Accessibility Tester:

- **IAAP:** go to accessibilityassociation.org/s/certification Once there, you can pick whether to get certified on CPACC, CPWA, WAS, ADS or CPABE. Getting certified in those will open many doors to accessibility testing jobs.

Performance Tester (CT-PT):

- **Edureka:** go to edureka.co and search for Performance testing, or the name of the app you want to learn related to it. For example, JMeter and you will get the courses related to teaching JMeter.

- **ISTQB:** go to istqb.org/certifications/performance-tester and get certified with them, which is the most common certification site but not as affordable as Edureka.

Mobile Tester:

- **ASTQB:** you can get the ISTQB Mobile Testing

Certification at <u>astqb.org/certifications/mobile-tester-certification/</u>

- **Edureka**: Go to <u>edureka.co</u> and type Mobile App Tester in the search box.

Security Tester (CT-ST)

- **ISTQB:** Go to <u>https://www.istqb.org/certifications/security-tester/</u> But before you can get the *Security Tester Certificate*, you need to have the CTFL one (Certified Foundation Level) from the same place.

- **Simplilearn**: If you go to <u>https://www.simplilearn.com/cyber-security-expert-master-program-training-course?tag=Securitytesting</u> you can get a *Cyber Security Expert Certification* where you'll learn CompTIA Security+, CompTIA Network+, ethical hacking and more.

- **GAQM:** Go to <u>https://gaqm.org/certification/software_security_testing</u> and you can get the *Certified Software Security Tester Certificate (CSST)* and *Certified Advanced Software Security Tester (CASST)* Certificate.

Resources

- Guru99.com was used for some definitions and exact lists, they have a lot of answers to common questions related to QA testing.

- For samples on Test cases, Test Plans, Resumes and blank templates visit this URL: https://bettertester.net/

- Great site for different types of QA testing information: softwaretestinghelp.com

- This site has some great learning resources as well https://www.tutorialspoint.com

- For Mobile Testing information specifically, go to this URL: softwaretestinghelp.com/best-mobile-testing-tools/

- Some of my favorite sites personally for learning are Udemy.com, Edureka.co and Codecademy.com

- For news and updates, sign up to these newsletters and follow them on social media:

testlio.com

MinistryofTesting.com

SoftwareTestingWeekly.com

Conclusion

Congratulations for making it this far! By now you should have a good idea on which QA specialty to concentrate on, and how to map out your path.

I hope this book helps you define your career and saves you time and money on deciding what to study next.

Don't forget Testers, especially female testers are far and few between, don't sell yourself short, and be courageous enough to apply for that job you think you meet only 50% of the requirements. I'd love to hear your stories and if this book helped you. Feel free to email me at bettertesterhelp@gmail.com, even if it's just to connect or say hello. I hope your Software QA journey is an exciting and successful one.

From one momma to another, I wish you the best!

Thank you and God bless,

Jennifer B.